TWENTY-DOLLAR BILLS

BY MADDIE SPALDING

The
Child's
World®
childsworld.com

Published by The Child's World®
1980 Lookout Drive • Mankato, MN 56003-1705
800-599-READ • www.childsworld.com

Photographs ©: Brian McEntire/Shutterstock Images, cover
(foreground), cover (background), 1 (foreground), 1 (background),
6, 7, 20 (top) 20 (bottom); Janusz Pienkowski/Shutterstock
Images, 5; Andreas Reh/iStockphoto, 9; Shutterstock Images,
11; iStockphoto, 13, 16; Joe Raedie/Getty Images News/Getty
Images, 15; Georgios Art/iStockphoto, 19; Red Line Editorial, 22

Design Elements: Brian McEntire/Shutterstock Images, Ben Hodosi/
Shutterstock Images

ISBN 9781503820111
LCCN 2016960504

Printed in the United States of America
PA02336

ABOUT THE AUTHOR

Maddie Spalding writes and
edits children's books. She lives in
Minnesota.

TABLE OF CONTENTS

CHAPTER ONE

WHAT IS A TWENTY-DOLLAR BILL?. . . . 4

CHAPTER TWO

SECURITY FEATURES. 8

CHAPTER THREE

THE HISTORY OF THE TWENTY-DOLLAR BILL 14

TIMELINE 20

FAST FACTS 21

WHERE MONEY IS MADE. . .22

GLOSSARY 23

TO LEARN MORE 24

INDEX 24

WHAT IS A TWENTY-DOLLAR BILL?

Twenty-dollar bills are a type of money. Four five-dollar bills equal one twenty-dollar bill. The Bureau of Engraving and Printing (BEP) makes twenty-dollar bills. Bills are made from cotton and **linen**.

The BEP makes more than eight billion twenty-dollar bills each year.

Andrew Jackson

Serial Number

Treasury Seal

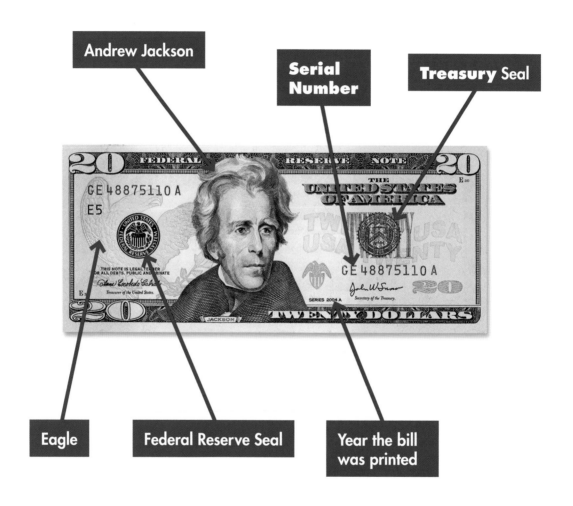

Eagle

Federal Reserve Seal

Year the bill was printed

Former president Andrew Jackson is on the front of the twenty-dollar bill.

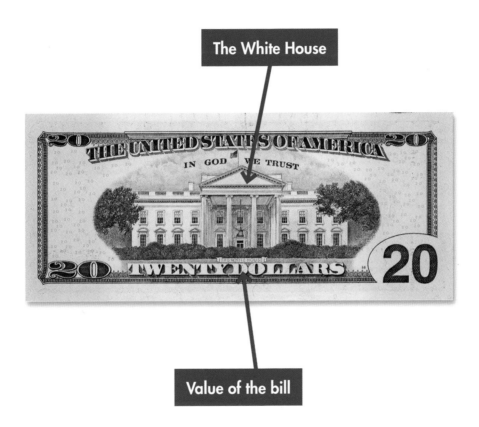

The White House

Value of the bill

The White House is on the back.

CHAPTER TWO

SECURITY FEATURES

Each twenty-dollar bill has a security thread. This thread glows green under **ultraviolet** light.

How are the images on the front and back of the twenty-dollar bill related?

Security threads are found on five-, ten-, twenty-, fifty-, and one hundred–dollar bills.

The twenty-dollar bill also has a hidden image. This is called a watermark. Another image of Andrew Jackson can be seen when the bill is held up to a light.

The watermark is in the blank space on the right side of the bill.

Each twenty-dollar bill has a different serial number. These security features make it more difficult for people to make fake twenty-dollar bills.

Which security feature do you think is the most useful? Why?

The green serial numbers help to identify which Federal Reserve Bank gave out the bill.

CHAPTER THREE

THE HISTORY OF THE TWENTY-DOLLAR BILL

The first U.S. twenty-dollar bills were made in 1861. A woman was on the front. Her name was Lady Liberty.

The U.S. Treasury is in charge of redesigning the twenty-dollar bill.

Grover Cleveland was both the 22nd and 24th president of the United States.

Grover Cleveland was put on the front of the twenty-dollar bill in 1914. He was president of the United States in the late 1800s.

Andrew Jackson first appeared on the twenty-dollar bill in 1929. The White House was put on the back of the bill that same year.

Why might the U.S. government have wanted to put Andrew Jackson on the twenty-dollar bill?

ANDREW JACKSON was the seventh president of the United States (1829–1831). He was also a commander in the U.S. Army.

1861 The first U.S. twenty-dollar bills were made. Lady Liberty was on the front.

1914 Grover Cleveland was put on the front of the twenty-dollar bill.

2004 U.S. twenty-dollar bill

1929 Andrew Jackson first appeared on the twenty-dollar bill.

1998 The U.S. Treasury began adding security features to the twenty-dollar bill.

Back of the 2004 U.S. twenty-dollar bill

★ The U.S. Treasury plans to reveal new designs for the twenty-dollar bill in 2020. Andrew Jackson will be moved to the back of the bill. Harriet Tubman will be put on the front.

★ Harriet Tubman was a former slave who helped many others escape slavery in the mid-1800s. She also fought for women's rights.

★ Many people do not want Andrew Jackson on the twenty-dollar bill because he forced tens of thousands of Native Americans to leave their homes in the 1830s. This was called the Trail of Tears.

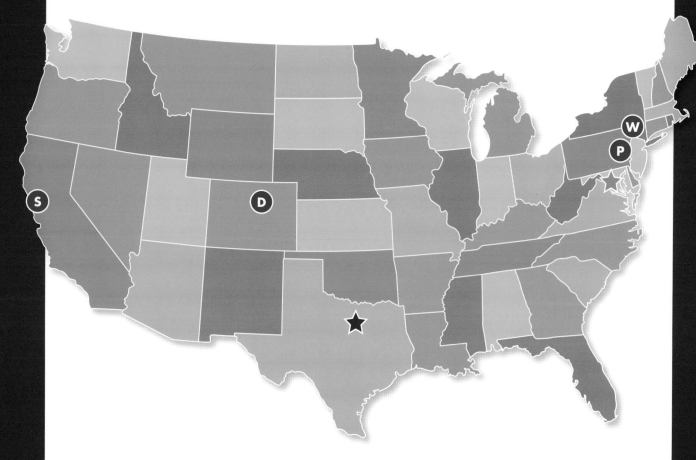

BUREAU OF ENGRAVING AND PRINTING OFFICES

★ Fort Worth, Texas

★ Washington, DC

COIN-PRODUCING MINTS

D Denver, Colorado—Produces coins marked with a D.

P Philadelphia, Pennsylvania—Produces coins marked with a P.

S San Francisco, California—Produces coins marked with an S.

W West Point, New York—Produces coins marked with a W.

linen (LIN-uhn) Linen is a strong type of cloth. Twenty-dollar bills are made from cotton and linen.

serial number (SEER-ee-ull NUM-bur) A serial number is a group of numbers that identifies something. Each twenty-dollar bill has a serial number.

Treasury (TREZH-ur-ee) A Treasury is a part of a government that is in charge of a country's money. The U.S. Department of the Treasury is in charge of money in the United States.

ultraviolet (uhl-truh-VYE-uh-lit) Ultraviolet is a type of light. Security threads on twenty-dollar bills glow green under ultraviolet light.

IN THE LIBRARY

Dowdy, Penny. *Money.* New York, NY: Crabtree, 2009.

Gregory, Josh. *Andrew Jackson: The 7th President.*
New York, NY: Bearport, 2015.

Pace, Lorenzo. *Harriet Tubman and My Grandmother's Quilts.*
New York, NY: Windmill Books, 2015.

Schuh, Mari C. *Counting Money.* Minneapolis, MN:
Bellwether, 2016.

ON THE WEB

Visit our Web site for links about
twenty-dollar bills: childsworld.com/links

Note to Parents, Teachers, and Librarians: We routinely verify our Web links to make sure
they are safe and active sites. So encourage your readers to check them out!

INDEX

Bureau of Engraving and
    Printing, 4
Cleveland, Grover, 17
cotton, 4
Federal Reserve Seal, 6
Jackson, Andrew, 6, 10, 18–19
Lady Liberty, 14
linen, 4

serial number, 6, 12
Treasury Seal, 6
ultraviolet, 8
watermark, 10
White House, 7, 18